Sunshine & Stagelights

story by Cara Hendrickson

illustrations by Cory Steiger

Copyright © 2024 The Full Monte LLC.

All rights reserved. This book or any portion thereof may not be reproduced or used in any manner whatsoever without the express written permission of the publisher except for the use of brief quotations in a book review.

Printed in the United States of America.

First printing, 2024.

www.runnkd.com

For Ashton, my sunshine

I have the distinct honor of watching my own heart outside my body singing, dancing and bringing light to this world. Your laugh is infectious and your spirit unwavering.

2 Timothy 1:7

I saw you today and it reminded me of what has brought you to this moment and the path we have been on together.

As I wait in anticipation of what you will do next,

I hope you know...

I saw you...

When the applause was quieter than you expected for the role you played.

I saw you...

The time you stumbled and fell. I saw how deeply it hurt you and how hard you worked to get back up and keep going.

I saw you..:

When you felt hurt and betrayed by the way they treated you.

I hope you know...

Light overcomes the dark. The light of a new day breaks the long hours of the night. One spark of love can break through the longest night and deepest darkness.

I hope you know...

I saw you all in all of those moments.

I want nothing more than for you to see me standing alongside you, for you to experience joy in the deepest parts of your heart, and how much I love you. The finish line of the journey will be worth it.

I cannot wait to watch you every step of the way with the same pride and excitement I have today.

Take time to pray today that the love of our Heavenly Father will wash over you:

Father, thank you for creating me, for believing in me, and for never being too far away. Remind me of your love in your quiet ways. This world and these moments are only part of your story. Remind me of my purpose to serve you and answer your call to use my gifts to share you love, glory, and promises with others.

Amen

About the Author

Cara is the mother of two and wife to her lifelong best friend, residing in Boerne, Texas.

Her stories are born out of the need to comprehend the world around and above her through an indulgence in written words, whether in the form of heartfelt letters, eulogies, short stories, poems, journaled rantings, short devotionals and hosts of anecdotal analogies.

Cara graduated from Penn State University in 2010 with a Master's Degree in Project Management and in 2002 with a Bachelor's Degree in Psychology. Her life mission is to author a series of works centered around her passion for connecting, celebrating and honoring others through words.

Discover more of Cara's work at RUNNKD
runnkd.com
@runnkd_life

Therefore, since we are surrounded by such a great cloud of witnesses, let us throw off everything that hinders and the sin that so easily entangles. And let us run with perseverance the race marked out for us. Hebrews 12:1

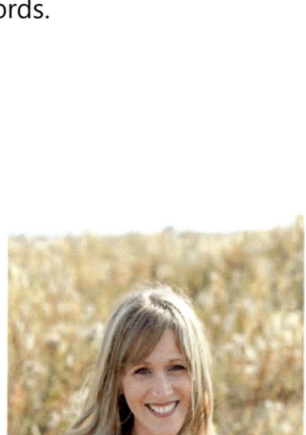

About the Illustrator

Cory is a gifted artist. When not creating illustrations for books, he designs and paints sets for musical theater productions. He is currently working on his Masters of Fine Art in Set Design at Temple University.

And if that weren't enough, he's a Board-Certified Behavior Analyst working to help children.

Discover more of Cory's work at CJS Designs, LLC
cjsdesignsme.com

Made in the USA
Columbia, SC
31 January 2024